TRUE LOVE THROUGH CONFLICT

≣**NOLO**
Publishers

ANDREW SPAUMER

ALL RIGHTS RESERVED. No part of this publication may be reproduced, stored in a retrieval system, or transmitted in any form or by any means – electronic, mechanical, photocopying, recording or otherwise – without written permission from the publisher, except per the provisions of the Copyright Act, 98 of 1978.

Copyright © 2018 Andrew Spaumer
Unless otherwise identified: All the definitions are taken from the Cambridge, and Urban Dictionary. All scripture quotations, are taken from the New King James Version (NKJV) of the Holy Bible. Copyright © 1982 Thomas Nelson. Inc. Words meaning and definitions included
True Love Through Conflict
ISBN-13: 978-0-620-81900-8

Publishers: Nolo Publishers
Cover design: Stanley Maake
Typeset in 9/12 Adobe Caslon Pro
Printed by Nolo Publishers 1 2 3 4 5 1 2

Every effort has been made to obtain copyright permission for the material used in this book. Please contact the author with any queries in this regard.

Conflict is an opportunity to learn to love our partner

better over time

~Dr Julie Gottman~

Dedication

To God the Father through the Lord Jesus Christ My Lord. These are the works of the Holy Spirit. I dedicate this book to my wife Nomsa Spaumer, and to my girl Nontobeko and my son Mofenyi. To every married couple and those aspiring to be married someday, this book is dedicated to empowering you as you strive to build solid relationships through conflicts. When I wrote this book, I had you in mind.

Table of Contents

Acknowledgments ii

Preface v

Chapter 1 True Love 9

Chapter 2 Conflict 26

Chapter 3 Conflict in Romantic Relationships 46

Chapter 4 Conflict in Marriage 58

Chapter 5 The Value of Conflict 75

Chapter 6 Handling Conflict 90

Chapter 8 Unresolved Conflict 116

Chapter 9 Negotiating Conflicts 125

References 149

Acknowledgments

I thank God for Jesus Christ who enabled me to complete this project. The message of hope and love found in the Bible was relevant when I received Jesus Christ as my Lord and Saviour in 1985. This message is still relevant even today. It is an honour to see the full manifestation of the Holy Spirit in my life every day.

To my mother, Ms Anna Motjetse Moshatane, you fought hard as a single mother to make sure that your three boys had a proper education and shelter over their heads. Your tears and hard work are rewarded daily. Thank you for your love and prayers. My younger brothers; Gibson Moshe Spaumer and Willem Spaumer, you are the best. I am proud to have you as my brothers; I could not have asked for more.

There are a lot of people who have contributed in one way or another for me to be where I am today. I wouldn't have made it this far without your help and encouragement.

There are pastors who have mentored and fathered me from the day I accepted Jesus Christ as my Lord and Saviour; I am grateful for your support God will reward you for watering my garden. El-Bethel Christian Fellowship, you are a group of winners and this is dedicated to you.

To all the couples and young people who have continually engaged my services as a Relationship Coach, thank you for confirming the calling upon my life; which is to transform relationships. To Professors Reineth and Gert Prinsloo, thanks for opening my eyes to the international world. This exposure could not have happened without all my sponsors and ministry partners.

Lastly, I want to thank my wife Mrs Nomsa Spaumer for her encouragement and work in making sure that this book is completed on time. Thank you for seeing the best in me when I was at my lowest and encouraging me to pursue my passion. To my children Nontobeko and Mofenyi, you are the best and thank you for sacrificing your time for me to achieve this project. Thank you for sharing me with the world, and you will be suitably rewarded.

Preface

We sometimes find ourselves in a romantic relationship with someone at some point in our lives. Being in love and being loved is the most beautiful thing that everyone should wish for and strive for. Love is a feeling that you can only experience if you have learnt to love and value yourself. True love starts with knowing yourself, accepting yourself for who you are and understanding your worth. The ability to love yourself gives you a better chance to love someone and to understand what love is.

When someone comes into your life, they should find you with some level of love that already exists within you. When their love connects with your existing love, it will be a continuation. The media has over the years influenced how love is defined and understood. The influence cannot be overlooked. We have been sold a picture of relationships that always start and end well "Happy ever after."

Conflict is unavoidable in any relationship. Those who make an effort to manage conflict in a relationship, find that it helps them to know their spouse or partner better. Conflict shows that each person comes into the relationship as an individual who has their dreams and aspirations. These dreams and aspirations are shaped by their upbringing, society and the company they keep.

Those who have managed to learn about managing conflict have found that conflict helps to build better relationships, while setting better foundations for the growth of the relationship.

True love doesn't happen right away; it is an ever-growing process. It develops after you've gone through many ups and downs, when you've suffered together, cried together, laughed together

~RicardoMontalban~

Chapter 1

✤

True Love

Falling in love is easy, as being attracted to someone and experience the feeling of euphoria. This feeling is something that can be described as 'falling in love'. The feeling can be easy as it comes with all excitement as you learn all about what makes the other person tick. In doing that, you are also exposing your heart to the person you fell in love with. Remember when you first dated your partner; your world unexpectedly changed. You experienced repeated patterns of excitement, and your world revolved around your partner and could not imagine your life without your partner. True love is when two people really feel

True Love Through Conflicts

affection for each other, even though they face challenges, but they find a way to make it work. Love is not based only on what I can gain from you more than what I can offer; everyone has the capability to give and receive love. The basis of true love is that couples should take time to learn what is important to their partner and what their love language is. That according to me, is the basis of true love.

Love is shown by being willing to sacrifice what is important to me for the sake of the one I love. This can be described as the kind of love that does not have conditions, without any expectation or limits attached to it. The kind of love that we all long for, where someone can love you without trying to change you. True love has the emotional element to it that the Urban Dictionary explains below:

'A feeling created when two souls are easily drawn together in life.' Once they are together, there is something created that is so beautiful and strong that people fear, admire, and envy. When you have found that

True Love

person, they suddenly become the world to you. They light your way through life and never give up when things get tough. You cannot help but put them on a pedestal of admiration, always complementing and telling them how absolutely amazing they are. Making a sacrifice for them is no struggle if that is what you know you must do to be together. All you will ever want is to be together. To cuddle in your true loves arms every night and wake up to their presence every morning. You know all the quirks, what they like and do not like, all their favourite places to be touched, rubbed or scratched. You want nothing more than to share a life, home and family in the guaranteed happiness of the future.

You can always say I love you and know deep down in your heart of hearts that it is so real. With that kind of love, you are strong enough to go through anything you are faced with, and it is all you will ever need. If the world stops spinning or if the sun ever shines again you will have that love.'

True Love Through Conflicts

When these kinds of emotions and connections develop between two people, it becomes a feeling that seems like it will last for eternity, but with times its authenticity is challenged or tested by other needs in life which lead to conflict. When you are falling in love, you do not think of the possibility that the person may break your heart. In some instances, you are blinded to some obvious flaws or even doing something that will irritate you.

Those who have fallen in love only see the best in each other and are willing to let go of some of the irritating things and often compromise in the name of love.

True Love

The feeling associated with being loved includes being appreciated, supported, heard, and knowing that you are special to the person who professes to love you. True love has more to do with the actions, than what one professes with their mouth. When you are loved you want to know that the person claiming to love you has your best interests at heart and vice versa. It may seem cliché to talk about how one will cross the oceans and climb the highest mountain for the one they love but such kind of promises leave one assured of love beyond what they can offer to the one they love.

True love talks beyond one's faults and shortcomings; it looks beyond the mistakes and sees the person who is loved. True love shows respect to the person being loved. Respect in any relationship is important for the sustenance of true love. In respecting each other, we understand that we are individuals with differences that work together to produce the chemistry that we both benefit from.

In true love, we accept each other with all the good and the bad attributes. We deal with each other with the grace and mercy because we understand that in as much as we can see our partners' faults; we also have our own faults which they are bearing with because they love us. In accepting each other, we put down all our preconceived ideas about each other and accept the true nature of who we are.

True Love Through Conflicts

We understand that we were brought up from different families with different values that we can agree on and build from there. We do not impose our values on each other, but we find a common understanding through the love we share. We experience true love through the deeds r than with uttered words.

Those who experience true love find that there is mutual respect between them. They know that they add value in each other's lives in their own unique way that the other person being loved cannot do without.

It is through true love that our wishes and feelings have value as they find acknowledgement from our partners. In acknowledging the wishes and feelings of your partner, you are letting your partner know that you are trying to keep their ideas and feelings in mind.

In making sure that true love sustains mutual respect, couples will need to learn to speak-up because this will help in making sure that they are clear about what they want and need. Do not assume your partner will read your mind to know what is important to you but in telling them what you want, you create a platform for mutual respect.

There is nothing as dangerous as love without respect because respect says you understand that your partner is unique. Respect in true love means freedom to be yourself and to be loved for who you really are. Respect becomes one of the pillars of true love as it gives those in love an opportunity to talk openly and honestly with each other. Respect allows couples to listen to each other and value each other's feelings and needs.

Mutual respect in a relationship means you do not treat one another in a rude and disrespectful manner. Where there is mutual respect in a relationship, there is no name-calling or insults, demeaning each other or talking sarcastically to each other or even avoiding or ignoring each other.

Mutual respect is taking the views and opinions of your partner seriously. Considering your partner before making decisions that will affect them and being actively interested in their life; it is part of reciprocal respect.

True Love Through Conflicts

Displaying that you are interested in their work, daily activities, and what interest them. In true love, respect doesn't just happen, but it is established over time through actions like being consistently considerate and valuing your partner's feelings and opinions.

Reciprocated respect in true love can be sustained when we learn to be inter-reliant in our relationships. When you reciprocate, it does not mean that you do not need your partner, but it shows that you mutually support each other. You can pursue your separate interests as individuals with unique abilities and interests.

Self-sustenance in a relationship helps in building admiration and more attraction from your partner.

Setting boundaries will help to sustain mutual respect in a relationship. Boundaries are your own set of rules and precincts which together as couples need to respect. In a healthy relationship, healthy boundaries are set and respected. There can never be mutual respect in any relationship if the golden rule of treating each other as you would like to be treated is not applied. It is easy for any person to want to reap what they did not sow, especially good things, while the same people will cry foul when they reap the right fruits according to their seeds that they will have planted.

You can lose respect in your true love if what you say is the opposite of what you do especially when we talk about true love. When you love your partner and keep your words, you will earn their respect. If you say there are repercussions for something, and you do not follow through, your partner will not take you seriously. If there are no consequences, exploitation should be expected. In the same breath, do not allow yourself to make promises you are not prepared to follow through. When you do not keep your promises, you will be letting your partner down and in order to build trust, you need to follow through on your word, which can strengthen your relationship.

Similarly, once you have built trust, it is important to be self-confident in order to build a healthy relationship.

True Love Through Conflicts

Self-confidence makes true love attractive as there is nothing more confident and attractive as somebody who knows what they deserve. There is no true love where your partner knows they can get away with anything. Lack of consequences can signal the absence of love and respect.

To experience the value of mutual respect in true love, you will need to respect yourself. You need to value yourself enough to be able to clearly communicate your needs and desires.

True Love: Acceptance

To experience true love couples will have to learn to accept their partners as they are, not as they wish them to be. I have seen and heard people talking about changing their partner once they are married and that potentially leads to unnecessary conflicts in marriages. True love will teach you that your partner is essential in your life in the way they are. It doesn't mean you have to agree with everything they say, do or believe. What you need to know and understand is that your partner is not you and was not raised by your parents.

Whatever your partner was before you met them is what attracted you to them; so, accept what they are as they have accepted who you are. Many couples pray to God and spend money trying to change their partner. I consider this to be zombifying their partner.

The ability to accept yourself as someone that has strong and weak points will help you to accept your partner with their strong and weak points. Mastering your partner's strong and weak points can make your relationship to experience another level of true love as you can complement each other rather than compete against each other. When you accept yourself, you will be able to state your wants, needs and desires while knowing that your partner may or may not be willing to fulfil them.

True Love: Self-Acceptance

The experience of true love starts with self-acceptance before you expect someone to accept you. Self-acceptance is a state where you become satisfied or happy

True Love Through Conflicts

with yourself. It is a level in your life where you are aware of your strengths and weakness, and you are proud of the former and acknowledge the latter. Self-acceptance says to you I have deficiencies and have made bad choices in life, while I may have misbehaved but am satisfied with myself. Those who have accepted themselves have self-understanding and know they are unique.

True Love will not flourish with people who are always criticising themselves and trying hard to solve all the defects in their lives while failing to tolerate themselves to be imperfect in some parts. Loving someone who is critical or confused about their identity and wish they were any different from who they are, can drain the love energy out of you.

As said above some behaviour is contagious and someone who does not accept themselves can contaminate your self-worth.

Someone who has found true love accepts the person they are in love with, with their positive and negative attributes. When we learn to accept ourselves, we find it

True Love

easy to accept someone we love because in true love, our perspectives are open for us to see and learn things, we would not have experienced. In true love, we learn to harmonise our differences without being judgemental as we become open to receiving and accepting love as it comes.

True Love: Selflessness or Self-Seeking

Love is a verb which means it is a doing word. We experience true love when we are not in it for what we can benefit but rather what we could offer to the person we love. Those who enjoy true love do not insist upon their own way or their own rights. True love sacrifices self and considers the interests of the other person (partner) ahead of yours. We are living in a generation where people are more concerned about themselves and what they can benefit and less of what they can contribute in relationships.

Self-seeking should not be found in true love. Rather, we should serve one another, bearing one another's burdens while looking for the interests of the person you love and

True Love Through Conflicts

care about. Where there is true love, the desire should always be to seek the wellbeing of your partner than yours. One will enjoy the benefits of true love, when they know that their partner does not seek their own advantage, comfort, ease, honour, pleasure, or profit but will rather sacrifice all the above for their benefit.

This is well balanced through the love we have for ourselves which we know how to pass on to our partner. In every relationship, every person should find real joy and contentment by learning to offer more than being fixated on what they can get out of it. A commitment to love involves a commitment to sacrifice. When a couple make a conscious decision to put the best interests of their relationship before their own personal interests, it will ultimately benefit their relationship.

True love will release you from preoccupation with yourself. We can only experience true love, when we have something to give; and for anyone to receive true love they must be willing to give true love.

True Love

In giving true love, we should always remember that we need to learn how to love our partner the way they want to be loved. We should not make assumptions of how best to love them.

True Love: Trust

True love is built on the foundation of trust because it makes a couple to feel vulnerable without being fearful or defensive. Trusting each other in a relationship is an assurance for being reliable, responsible and dependable. Trust in true love means that I can rely on my partner as I have confidence in them because I am feeling physically and emotionally confident. Trust is essential for true love because you cannot love someone you do not trust especially because you are in a vulnerable position when you are in love.

To know that you have someone you trust, and that they have your best interests at heart, boosts your confidence to open your heart for more love. When you have trust in your relationship you are sure that you will not fight your battles alone. Trust in a relationship makes a couple

True Love Through Conflicts

to be more positive and optimistic especially amid conflicts. Trusting each other in a relationship gives a couple an opportunity to grow and flourish because failing to trust your partner can result in one censoring them.

Conflict is inevitable, Combat is optional

~Max Lucado~

Chapter 2

❦

Conflict

Conflict can be described as a serious disagreement or argument which can last longer than expected or usual. We are looking at a conflict that is interpersonal as we talk about the conflict in a romantic relationship. It can also be described as a dispute, quarrel, squabble, disagreement or difference of opinions. A conflict between two people can lead to a fight or an argument. Conflict between people who love each other can be caused amongst other things by personality differences.

True Love Through Conflicts

The other thing that can lead to conflict is clashes in emotional needs. When two people come into a loving relationship, the focus can be more on the things that make them to be attracted to one another.

During the time when the focus is on the things that make them be attracted to each other, they can miss the opportunity to learn about things that make them different. This stage can be described as the honeymoon stage in a relationship.

The honeymoon period describes the beginning stage in a relationship, when it feels fresh and exciting; a time when a lot of new things are learnt about each other. Conflict in a relationship will come as the couple's excitement about each other fades away, and because of the time they have spent with each other and the activities they have engaged together, boredom may lead to questioning one's feelings.

Conflict happens in a relationship when there is a sense of struggle or incompatibility or perceived differences. This can emanate from differences in values, desires or

Conflict

goals that two people had before coming into a relationship and as the relationship develops. Conflict is related to action or expression because until there is action or expression, the relationship can look normal. It is without a doubt that during conflict, couples try to show power or attempt to influence each other to a view.

In an attempt to influence or show power, if the other party does not care about the outcome, their discussion will not qualify to be called a conflict. This can be considered as a disagreement, as the two people arguing do not care about what happens next nor do they seek to engage with each other.. Conflict cannot be a breakdown in communication, as it should be a process that is ongoing.

Conflict instead, entails communication about what the couple disagrees about. Couples should understand that conflict is not inherently good or bad even though we are more likely to remember only the painful experiences as a result of or that led to conflict. Conflict is normal in any human interaction as it helps in building stronger

True Love Through Conflicts

bonds. We should never make the mistake of thinking that communication will automatically resolve any conflict. We should know that to have the best outcome out of any conflict, you will require conflict management skills.

One of the well-researched causes of conflict in any form of relationship has been found to be poor communication. When expectations are not well communicated it can lead to arguments and fights in a relationship. People who love each other come together to meet the needs that they have for each other and for the time they are together they can meet the needs; but when they differ, and conflict arises, there is a threat to their needs, interests, and concerns not being met. When we consider conflict in relationships, it is important to note that we are not just talking about a disagreement between two people in love, but a situation where a spouse perceives a threat (physical, emotional, power, status) which might threaten their well-being.

Conflict

As explained in the Maslow's hierarchy of needs (Vinney, 2018), human draws motivation when their basic needs (physiological, safety, belonging and love, esteem and self-actualisation) are met and when those basic needs are not met even in a relationship, it has the potential to lead to conflict. It is in every human being to want to meet his/her needs, and for the motivation to occur at the next level, each level must be satisfied within the individual. A relationship with someone you truly love should serve to motivate you to meet those needs further.

Conflict in a relationship often starts due to different ideas and goals in a relationship. When needs (expected) are not met this can lead to conflict. These situations are made complex when one spouse feels unheard or overseen in the relationship. Couples who do not have a common understanding about certain things in their relationship, like how to spend money, house chores, how to spend time together or even how the other spouse wants to be loved, expose themselves to the inevitable -

confrontation and conflict with irreversible damage in some instances.

When spouses fail to clearly communicate their expectations in a relationship, they raise their hopes with unfair expectations and this often leads to conflict between two people who truly love each other. The other important cause of conflict in a relationship can be power plays and manipulation in the relationship.

There are different factors that can cause conflict in relationships. We are going to look at some of these factors as explained by Dr David Burns in his book "Feeling Good Together". Dr Burns mentions some of the causes of conflicts in relationships as:

Power and control: it is normal for people to want to have superiority over others as this gives them an opportunity to get what they want from the relationship. Some people use intimidation in relationships to have power and control over their partners. In such cases, couples fail to show empathy and respect for each other as intimidation within the relationship drives out intimacy.

Self-Blame: people who always blame themselves for everything that goes wrong in a relationship without taking time to appreciate the good things they are contributing can drain the relationship to its early grave. Self-blame can take a lot of energy out of you that other people may feel uncomfortable to be around you. A couple needs to equally take responsibility for things going wrong in their relationship and take an adult, neutral stance rather than an emotionally charged one.

Revenge: When you are in a relationship and you are always driven by the desire to prove a point; be careful as this will kill the passion of love. Revenge comes when we always seek our way and fail to accept our partner's views. We must always remember that the joy of revenge is short lived as we feel righteous for some time before we start being anxious about what the other party is planning for revenge. Revenge can protract conflict because no one wins, and no one wants to stop. It takes maturity to give-in to break the cycle.

Justice and fairness: I often hear people saying; 'it is not fair' when they actually mean is 'this is not what I want'. It is easy to get consumed by pain and assume that your feelings reflect the way things are supposed to be even for our partner. When you feel entitled to justice and fairness, your belief is that it is your partner who needs to change. With this belief, you feel entitled to continue your hurtful behaviour. It is when you are angry with your partner that your mind is filled with all the negative thoughts which in that moment seem valid. When you - reflect on our thoughts while angry, it's most likely that you will realise some errors in your judgement.

Conflict can come when we try to defend ourselves from criticism that we may perceive as irrational or unfair; you instantly prove it to be valid. If you agree with it, you prove it wrong. Try to think of a time when your partner has said to you "you never listen to me" and you

Conflict

responded with 'you might be right about that'. That kind of response shows that you were listening.

Competition: it is the desire of everyone to be the best in the game, and it is this desire that makes us be competitive and want more challenges. When a couple chooses to compete instead of complimenting each other, it leads to conflicts. The competition will even affect how they manage conflict as each will like to have the last word in any arguments or difference.

Anger and bitterness: when you are angry you express it actively by seeking or avoiding confrontation. The best advice will be to calmly and respectfully share your feelings.

Blame: when you play the blame game in a relationship, you do not take responsibility. You look for anything possible for you to escape and this can leave your partner hostile towards you. Those people who do not want to take the blame do not see a need for them to change.

Scapegoating: For some people, when you raise an important matter in a relationship, they start labelling you as inferior or defective which in-turn clears them for all the wrongs in the relationship. Without evidence, you try to find something wrong with your partner which you can use against them. When there is nothing, you can even start reinforcing the lie through gossip and repeating the lie, the process you secretly enjoy.

Pride and Shame: when you are wrong, and you know your faults, but you undermine the views of your partner. This can lead you to be hostile towards them. If we want to build a strong intimate relationship, we will need to allow ourselves to be vulnerable because true intimacy requires us to confront our failings.

Truth: as put by St. Augustine 'we love the truth when it enlightens us; we hate the truth when it convicts us.' It is easy to celebrate the truth and demand it from our spouse, but when the truth is denied, it can cause conflict. What hurts the most in a relationship is when the truth is intentionally withheld.

Conflict starters in a relationship

Conflict

Conflict in relationships starts when you become selfish and more absorbed with what you think you deserve without considering the needs of your partner. In a relationship, one can get obsessed with what they need that they cease to care about they do it. When you are in a relationship, it is no longer just about you and what you need. You will need to remember that your decisions have an impact on your partner too. Failing to be to be considerate to your partner's needs, can dampen true love. What can be more painful is when your partner purposefully becomes selfish by making decisions knowing that they may have detrimental effects on you. True love is not self-seeking and when you become selfish in the relationship you clearly show that you do not respect your partner. Paul says in Philippians 2:3

> *"Let nothing be done through selfish ambition or conceit, but in lowliness of mind let each esteem others better than himself."*

True Love Through Conflicts

If this principle applies to every human interaction, then it will be more appropriate where two people claim to love each other. Conflict starts when we become selfish and seek to benefit more than we give.

When we fail to communicate properly, it can lead to misunderstandings that can lead to conflict within the relationship. Someone said what you are saying is as important as how you are saying it. It is when we feel that we are not listened to, that we end-up using violence to be recognised. We resort to unconventional ways in order to be heard and that causes conflict with our partners. When couples reach a dead end in their communication, it can lead to tensions. Failure to communicate leads to assumptions which then lead to wrong needs being met by your partner.

When we fail to communicate what has hurt us to our partner, we tend to keep the painful emotions in the heart that are supposed to be poured out. The more we are thinking about the pain caused, the more we become resentful. Resentment against our partner can easily

Conflict

create distance, loss of interest in important things and bad vibe in the relationship. Because the other party may not know that they have done something wrong, they can also block their partner out which escalates the conflict even further.

Conflict in relationships is inevitable when we give the responsibility of our joy to our partner. It is important that it is your happiness that makes the relationship a happy one. When we wait for our partners to make us happy, we become frustrated when they fail to meet our needs. We enter relationships with expectations that are unrealistic and when they are not met, we get frustrated which is a recipe for conflict.

Conflict in a relationship can also be caused by assumptions. An assumption can be defined in the dictionary as 'a thing that is assumed to be true.' When we come into a relationship, we come with certain assumptions which we have built over time and we believe them to be true. It is when these assumptions are challenged that tensions may rise to cause conflict.

True Love Through Conflicts

What makes conflict worse is making we assumptions about our partner's intentions, reasons for action, or their understanding of the situation. Failure to check or identify our assumptions and giving our partner an opportunity to give their own interpretation of situations can lead to conflict in relationships.

On the other hand, perception is defined as 'a way of regarding, understanding or interpreting something.' Though we might be madly in love, we each have our own perceptions on certain matters that are important to us. People's perceptions are shaped by their assumptions, expectations, experiences and history.

Conflict in a relationship can be triggered by failing to be open about how we perceive different issues and adjust our perception through the new information we receive from our partner.

We all grow up with certain expectations which we adopt as we grow up and interact with other people. These expectations have also influenced the way we look at roles that each partner must play in the relationship.

Conflict

Some of the expectations have been taken from the stories we grow up listening to; while some from the couples we grow up admiring. When these expectations become normalised in us, we sometimes fail to communicate them when we develop relationships.

I have found that the worst expectations to triumph over are those we adopt from our immediate family members, particularly, our parents. It would seem normal to expect your partner to do these without asking questions.

The challenge is when questions are asked and reasons for such decisions are required, a couple can find themselves having to manage conflict in their relationship.

Conflict in relationships can also be caused by our personal history or should I say the journey that each partner in the relationship has travelled in the past. . Whatever we come across in life influences the way we think and act or even love. Previous love relationships can influence some of the decisions you may make in

True Love Through Conflicts

your current relationship, especially when you feel that you were hard done by your ex-partner.

There is a tendency to get into a new relationship with certain reservations to protect yourself from the pain that you might have gone through in your previous relationship. The sad thing is that your current partner; who was not part of your history might have to deal with things that they do not have an idea of. This might cause a strain in your relationship which can result in conflict.

The other example that comes to mind when talking about the background history in cases where one was abused or has experienced domestic violence. Even though you might have spoken about your experiences with your partner and they understand where you came from, certain actions from your partner can trigger those flashbacks. Your partner might not know how to handle your history. Certain behaviours or actions by your partner might remind you of the horrifying experience you have been through and it might cause conflict in your relationship.

Conflict

I have found that most couples have experienced cheating in their relationships before and when they come into a new relationship. This results in them being too cautious about their partner cheating. They become suspicious of every move their partner makes. Lack of trust within the relationship can make one paranoid and insecure. Being suspected of doing something you have not done has the potential to cause conflict in a relationship. The other partner might feel that they are being punished for what they do not know and while the one doing the monitoring feels that they cannot just trust anyone again due to what they have been through.

If you have been in a difficult financial position or you have grown up in a poor family, you might have a different relationship with money than the person who grew-up having enough in their family and their life in general. How couple spends their money can cause conflict in a relationship, not because they do not love each other but because of how they are different in how they spend money.

True Love Through Conflicts

Conflict in a relationship can be a result of failing to set boundaries on friends and family's involvement in a relationship. There are relationships where friends take more time and space more than the love relationship. On the other hand, you will find that there are relationships where the family members get too involved that they sometimes take over the relationship.

This can cause a strain between the couple especially the one feeling overburdened and not having space in the relationship. Some parents do this with a good motive as they want to protect their children or want what is best for their children, but this can, in turn, backfire when it causes conflict in a relationship.

Conflict

"The moment when we feel we must protect ourselves is usually the same moment when we harm our partners the most"

~Eric Michael Cohen~

Chapter 3

❧

Conflict in Romantic Relationships

When two people who are coming from different backgrounds come together into a romantic relationship, they are bound to have differences in opinions and ways of doing things. No matter how much the two can be in love, there are going to be places where they are going to have a different perspective on certain things. The ability to manage conflict well in the beginning stage of the relationship can raise the level of commitment in a relationship. You can avoid conflict in a relationship by relegating the responsibility of running the relationship to your partner.

When the love between two people is based on the resources, the one who is the beneficiary can lose their voice in the relationship with the fear of the benefits being withdrawn. One example of such a situation is seen in relationships between young men or women with older men or women (sugar daddies and sugar mamas). These older people will lavish the young woman/men with gifts in exchange for the company or sexual favours. Such kinds of relationships are not based on true love but on what one is benefitting from the relationship. Once the benefits are no longer available, this can lead to conflict in a romantic relationship.

There are situations where one might not be providing any material needs, but dominating and controlling the relationship. This controlling, in turn, leads to the other party surrendering their ability to contribute towards the direction of the relationship to the person who is dominating. The more one party loses their voice in a

Conflict in Romantic Relationships

relationship, under the impression that they are avoiding conflict, the more it leads to two people living one person's life. When one person loses their voice, it can lead to resentfulness, hurt and depression. This has the potential to lead a person to feel empty inside when everyone assumes, that they are loved and happy.

Within the religious community, especially amongst Christians, there is great pressure on relationships and marriage, which is exerted on young people. Being in a romantic relationship is considered a great achievement. To be involved with someone who is in a leadership position like the youth leader or worship team leader is considered an achievement. That comes with certain expectations, for example, to be in a romantic relationship and such pressure can lead people to get into romantic relationships even when they are not ready.

Christianity preaches submission and peace; and it is easy to be swayed to believe that conflict is 'evil' and some would foolishly choose to ignore conflict in their relationships. This is a ploy to cover up in order to make

True Love Through Conflicts

the relationship seem as to be 'working'. Conflict situations that are ignored in the courtship stage have the potential to escalate and cause cracks in marriages. The more conflict is ignored in the early stages of a relationship, the more a couple will grow distant even in marriage. Conflicts that come during dating or courtship can bring the couple even closer if managed effectively.

Couples who are in courtship but lack the capacity to manage their conflict successfully, consistently and systematically, I would say they are not ready to get married. The ability to have conflict and how it is managed should be a clear indication that the couple is ready to move to the level of marriage. Some people decide to get married because they do not have conflict in their relationship. This is a clear sign of a weak foundation even before the house is built. To build a strong house that will stand all the kinds of storms and winds, there is a need to dig deep into the foundation. Conflict is one of the best tools to assess if the foundation of your relationship is strong enough to hold in marriage.

Conflict in Romantic Relationships

I cannot emphasise the fact that conflict in any relationship is unavoidable and no matter how much you love each other you are going to have it. To have the skill to manage conflict as a couple before marriage is essential. Conflict management is an important tool in your marriage tool box as it will help you keep your relationship intact particularly in trying times. Conflict in any relationship exposes the level of respect that you have for each other. Where there is respect, a couple will be able to work together to come up with a conflict management style that will work for them.

Conflict during courtship

Dating can be explained as a time where two individuals are in the process of knowing each other. They can do this by doing some activities together like going for movies, having dinner or even cooking a meal together. There is no commitment or a romantic relationship going on between the two at this stage, but just a process of spending time together. There is no form of

True Love Through Conflicts

commitment during the dating period, and both individuals know that this can stop at any time.

During dating, the couple knows that their options of seeing other people are still open. On the other hand, courtship can be explained as a stage in the romantic relationship where the two individuals are committed to one another. At this stage, they are working towards engagement and marriage. The option of being involved with another person is not considered. During dating, there are no expectations from the relationship as the intention is just to have fun and see where the relationship might take them. The commitment associated with courtship or engagement in a romantic relationship can lead to some conflict that must be managed effectively to the preservation of true love shared by the two.

Courtship or engagement is not marriage, and this should give the couple an opportunity to know each other. During the period of engagement, there are opportunities for couples to experience conflicts as each

Conflict in Romantic Relationships

decides on things that will make them happy. I will not talk about the wedding day which on its own can create opportunities for conflict that can tell you more about the future of the couple in marriage. Conflict has within it, opportunities for the couples to know each other.

In his book "Things I Wish I'd Known Before We Got Married" Dr Gary D. Chapman speaks about a few things that are important to know and invest in before marriage. I have found the book to be an interesting read and will recommend every person who has found True Love to invest in it, as it will be an investment in their love. (Relationship, 2018) Here are the twelve things as taken from the book, "Things I Wish I'd Known Before We Got Married" (Dr. Gary, 2018).

❧ Feelings of being in love cannot sustain a marriage since the average life-span of these feelings is about two years. What sustains a marriage is when couples learn to communicate love in the forms that are most received and understood by their partner.

True Love Through Conflicts

❧ We will often develop weird similarities to our parents, even their drinking habits, communication patterns, energy levels, and appearances.

❧ Resolving marital disagreements without arguing. Truly listening to the other spouse in order to give an adequate summary of his or her perspective. Agreeing to disagree. Learning to compromise.

❧ The importance of spouses apologising for wrongdoing. Learning to speak your spouse's language of apology is more effective than just saying you are sorry. The five different ways of apologising are:

- Expressing regret
- Accepting responsibility
- Making restitution
- Genuinely expressing the desire to change your behaviour
- Requesting forgiveness

❧ Forgiveness is one's decision to offer grace instead of demanding justice.

Conflict in Romantic Relationships

- How spouses can agree on doing which household chores
- How spouses can most effectively manage their money and what common major mistakes to avoid, such as purchasing a home they cannot afford, going out to eat often, buying new cars, and buying too much alcohol. How you live on 80% of your income, give 10% to charity and save 10%. How couples can agree not to buy something over a certain amount consulting the other.
- Resolving common sexual difficulties. Overcoming the myth that partners must reach climax together. A husband should spend enough time caressing his wife. A husband participating in household chores will often increase desire in his wife for him. Spouses should only engage in sexual acts they are both comfortable with.
- How spouses can develop a good relationship with their in-laws, by learning to listen empathetically to them, speaking their love language to them, and alternating holidays with them

True Love Through Conflicts

ઓ Spiritual compatibility in marriage has more to do with what each spouse believes in the way God speaks to them and what He has said.

ઓ How spouses can live with a partner who has very different habits, including morning person versus night person, optimist versus pessimist, neat versus messy, talker versus non-talker, passive versus aggressive, logical thinker versus intuitive person, and organiser versus spontaneous person.

ઓ Having a balanced dating relationship by attending to these areas of growth: Intellectual, Emotional, Social, Spiritual and Physical.

Conflict in Romantic Relationships

"The extent to which two people in a relationship can bring up and resolve issues is a critical marker of the soundness of a relationship."

~ Henry Cloud ~

Chapter 4

❧

Conflict in Marriage

It is common to experience conflict in marriage, and the causes of disagreement vary from relationship to relationship. Conflict is inevitable in every marriage; you cannot completely escape from conflict it is therefore important to learn the skill and ways to manage it. The problem is not the conflict but how it is managed.

Conflict management is a life skill that every couple needs to learn; is it unfortunate that this so important skill is not taught in our school curriculum. Our ignorance is exposed by our encounter with situations that end up in conflict; we then realise how little we know about managing conflict in our relationships. How

Conflict in Marriage

you manage conflict in marriage determines the survival of your marriage.

Conflicts can also be caused by the different perspectives on issues, and in some instances, conflicts occur when one partner insists upon having his or her own way. This is when one partner insisting on having their own way at the expense of the other partner's happiness.

Having your own way at the expense of your partner will weaken your relationship over time. Other conflicts are caused purely as a result of unmet expectations. When expectations are not met, it leads to frustrations and a sense of not being valued in marriage. Conflicts can take many shapes and forms; they need to be managed well for the survival of a relationship and marriage.

As I was writing this book, I had several opportunities to put what I am writing into practice in my marriage. It dawned on me that writing about conflict, reading about conflict and talking about conflict is way more different than resolving the actual conflict in your personal relationship. You will never know how mature you are in

True Love Through Conflicts

this area until you go through the practice of managing real conflict in your marriage.

The value of a few conflict experiences during my writing has enhanced my writing and brought the subject closer home.

The value of successfully resolving conflict in your marriage outweighs the pain and emotions that you go through during the conflict. Conflict in a relationship gives you an opportunity to know your partner in a deeper level and learn what is important to your spouse and what his or her priorities are. This can happen if conflict is appropriately handled and it can lead to fulfilment as both parties reach a win-win situation. If one partner wins, you both lose, as you cannot have a fulfilled relationship if one partner feels like they have lost.

Fighting in marriage

As human beings, we all have needs and these are essential for a fulfilled marriage. Not acknowledging

Conflict in Marriage

those needs can also be part of the problem as that may mean that we may fail to communicate those needs to our spouse and failure may result in an unfair expectation that your spouse will be expected to know and even fulfil those needs that are not communicated.

The uncommunicated needs are an underlying factor to most marital conflicts. When one spouse feels that he or she is not cared for in the way he wants that can lead to disappointments. Knowing your needs and communicating them openly and honestly to your spouse is critical to alleviating potential conflict in marriage. It is essential that is clear in your mind, or that you are aware of your needs, you communicate them and give your spouse an opportunity to meet them.

Although it should be noted that it an unrealistic expectation to presume that another human being will meet all your needs, this should not be mistaken as making your spouse responsible for your happiness. You are always responsible for your own happiness. There are reasonable expectations that as married couples we need to ensure that those basic needs are met for both spouses to feel safe and secure.

We often say that love conquers all; with the thinking that love is all you need in your marriage. We put our energy into ensuring that we maintain love without focusing on the basic needs that will nurture the marriage and make it blossom. As couples if our basic needs are not met, it leads to protracted conflict that in turn cause partners to feel neglected, unsafe and frustrated. In most instances, partners are not keen to ask for what they want. Once you have threads of conflict that you are not able to determine the source, it could be as a result of a suppressed unmet need.

Conflicts is a challenging part in relationships; it is in some instances caused by the deprivation of human basic needs in a relationship. It can be valuable to determine some causes of conflict if the conflict is as a result of unmet human needs.

Value of Healthy Conflict in Marriage

Conflict in Marriage

Marriage is the joining together of two different individuals in a bond that is generally considered to last till death. This bond is between two people who have different family backgrounds, diverse life experiences, who look at things differently and in most cases, have a different outlook on life; therefore, conflict under such circumstances is inevitable. It is also important to look out for behavioural patterns amongst couples that are a fertile ground for couples to experience unhealthy conflict. Healthy marriages not about being the same but it is about the ability to navigate and respond well to your differences.

The closeness we experience in marriage reveals what matters to us and the weaknesses that we never knew existed. Marriage can be a mirror image of who you really are. When living alone you do not have to deal with in-laws, marriage expectations, emotional work of calming spouse's bruised feelings or even account to someone else about your whereabouts or your expenditure.

True Love Through Conflicts

All these can be a source of conflict in marriage as your priorities may not be the same around these issues. There are some things that are important to you that you can realise until you are in a married. Marriage can reveal the 'blind spots' that you may not be aware of. Conflict presents an opportunity for couples to learn more about one another and calls for partners to accept that they are two different individuals. It helps couples to embrace their individuality and make their differences work for them not against them which in turn create synergy.

For conflict to add value, and bring closeness to couples, they need to have a resolve to make the relationship work. The married couple should be willing to make some sacrifices for the benefit or success of the relationship even if it means not getting their own way.

Couples who are willing to sacrifice can manage their conflicts effectively. Through conflict, they are able to experience more closeness and fulfilment - as the spouses feel that their relationship is safe to express their feeling, their fears and work through them in a loving environment. They know that in a marriage relationship, they cannot always get their way, but they are committed enough to do what it takes to make the marriage successful.

When the partners are in conflict, they have few choices on how to respond. The response to conflict is the determining factor if your conflict will add value or will disconnect you to your partner. A healthy conflict has a potential for bringing bliss in your marriage and creating a safe environment.

In a relationship where couples are too cautious to avoid conflict, or perceive conflict as 'bad' for their relationship; you will find that disagreements are avoided at all costs to keep peace at the expense of happiness. There is a tendency to sweep issues under the carpet rather than confronting them. In this way, issues will not be resolved not will they go away.

You can manipulate your spouse to have your way, avoid conflict or even ignore it, which will not resolve it until you face it head-on. The buried conflict can grow to the extent that you cannot tolerate it anymore, explode and destroy your family.

The absence of conflict may not necessarily be the presence of peace or an indicator of happiness in a relationship or marriage. It may signal hardened hearts, or maybe one spouse may feel unsafe to express his/her needs and value. Such a spouse can suppress or keep peace at all cost by giving in to the needs of the other spouse.

Couples that are in a healthy relationship use conflict to enhance their bond and connection. They understand that conflict is not signalling the end of a relationship. Each spouse feels safe to speak their concerns, and they differ without calling them names. That increases the level of security in a relationship.

The best gift you can give to your relationship is being a safe place without trying to change your partner but rather trying to understand them and their world, which will make your marriage to flourish.

Unhealthy conflict

Conflict in Marriage

How you see conflict as a couple plays a huge role in how the conflict will be handled. Do you see it as the end of a relationship? Do you see it as good or bad? Do you see it as something that serves you or works against you, do you use conflict as an aid to go into each other's world and understand better by seeing the other partner's perspective? Are you viewing conflict as less threatening to the relationship and perceive the relationship to be a safe place for exploration?

It is important for couples when experiencing conflict to understand that healthy conflict is common and essential in a marriage to a certain degree. The key to a fulfilling marriage is not a complete elimination of conflict; it is the he ability to effectively manage conflict which helps to bring satisfaction in marriages.

As much as the right dose of conflict is acceptable, a couple should guard against constant bickering. Conflict becomes unhealthy when it starts to dominate the bigger part of your relationship to the extent that as a couple, you cease to be civil with each other. It should be a concern when one resents being at their marital home or feeling like tons of bricks are placed on your shoulder because you know that the first conversation you will have with your spouse will set the house on fire. In such cases, you really need to take stock and reflect on the underlying reasons for such intense conflict levels.

If you keep on biting and devouring each other, you need to be careful that you do not destroy one another. That kind of conflict will not build understanding or closeness but will lead to a dysfunctional marital relationship to the extent of damaging your true love. It is not easy to measure the right dose of conflict necessary for any relationship or to determine the threshold for a healthy relationship as that will be dependent on each family dynamics and phase in their relationship.

Conflict is unhealthy when the following common mistakes are committed

Involving children: As indicated that conflict is inevitable in a marriage relationship, meaning a marriage relationship will not be completely free from

Conflict in Marriage

disagreement and conflict. It is important to consider how kids are impacted when their parents are in a high conflict relationship. Kids suffer when their parents argue. It is even worse when partners use kids to discredit one another to fight their battles. This in turn pollutes and confuses the innocent mind of a child.

The child may end up blaming himself or herself for their parents' disagreement. It is therefore important not to manipulate children and drag them into your relationship conflict. This can damage the children emotionally and psychologically. It threatens their safe family environment due to the frequency of the conflict between spouses, especially when it is accompanied by shouting, insults and physical aggression.

What you display to your children during disagreements is important in creating a safe environment for them. The aim should not be to totally shield children from seeing their parents disagree or in conflict but to show the kids that it is okay to disagree and how to effectively respond to conflict in such a way that it does not destroy the relationship.

The objective is for children to see their parents relate to each other during the heated argument by responding positively and peacefully. Children need to see their parents managing conflict together and this, in turn, gives them an opportunity to learn the best way of responding to conflict without breaking down relationships.

Involving Family members: Inviting family members into your marriage during conflict may have a far-reaching impact than it is anticipated. Sometimes couples goes through conflict, or they just want to vent out about the conflict they had with family members. The more you continue doing this, you are creating a negative impression to your family about your spouse. No matter how trivial the argument is, always remember the saying that "blood is thicker than water" meaning family relationships and loyalties are strong.

Conflict in Marriage

Even though you and your partner may "kiss and makeup", the in-laws because of their loyalty to their son or daughter, may keep a record of the wrongs and may never forget that you once hurt their child. Family members may not forgive easily even years after the couple has dealt with the conflict. This may cause long term family divisions.

To avoid a situation where one person in the marriage dies silently, it will be important that as a couple you establish a strong support system around you. The risk of involving family members in every argument is that their emotional involvement may be biased. There are situations that may need the intervention of the family elders "*Malume*" uncles as we call them in South Africa. As a couple, you will know the level of conflict that requires family intervention.

Under normal circumstances, you and your spouse should keep your disagreements and conflict between the two of you. There will be instances where a third party may be necessary. It is advisable to seek support from a marriage counsellor, church leaders or trusted couples that you look up to and have both agreed to be your mentors.

This will also help in creating healthy boundaries with the close family members. It will also help to avoid having each family member having an opinion on how you should run your family. In turn, it will help in keeping the trust and ensuring that your marriage remains safe and conflict is managed effectively.

Punishment through denying sex or finances: When there is conflict in a marriage, it could impact the sexual desire. Denying your spouse sex to punish them over conflict is damaging to your marriage. I will consider that as being manipulative. Once sex is used as a punitive measure in a marriage, it leads to early death of the marriage. Sometimes, you see one partner leaving the marital bed and sleeps on the couch after conflict. Such behaviour leads to disconnection sexually over time. It is therefore important for couples to resolve conflict as soon as it arises, never let it compound to such an extent that it affects your sexual life. During conflict, it is important to have an attitude that your private parts are not part of the conflict. Sexual intimacy is protected when couples make an honest effort to create an emotionally safe environment in their marriage.

Marriage is an important institution for a couple to grow together. It also provides a good environment for the upbringing of the children. When couples learn the skills to manage conflict, they transfer those skills to their children.

"**Mankind** must evolve for all human conflict a method which rejects revenge, aggression, and retaliation. The foundation of such a method is love"

~Martin Luther King Jr~

Chapter 5

The Value of Conflict

Conflict in a relationship provides a chance to analyse the situation objectively while evaluating your needs as a couple. It provides an opportunity for the couple to come up with solutions that help them move towards a stronger relationship, with creative solutions and clear communication. Conflict in a relationship is not bad, but how you handle it can cause problems in the relationship. We will have conflict in a relationship because we chose to confront issues instead of pushing them under the rug or stuffing hurt feelings. Let us look at some of the important benefits of conflict in enhancing true love.

True Love Through Conflicts

When couples fail to address small things in a relationship, it can result in those things evolving into big matters hard to resolve in the future. Conflict gives an opportunity to address matters in the relationship that couples find hard to address. When we learn to address small uncomfortable things in a relationship, we create an opportunity to address bigger issues which are likely to show up later.

Couples can have many conflicts in their relationship about different things, which should not be a problem. The problem will be more on how they handle conflict more than the frequency of the conflict. Conflict should not be a problem in any relationship but how you address the conflict will determine the life-span of the relationship.

Benefits of conflict in a relationship

Conflict offers couples an opportunity to discover the great love and understanding they have for each other. There is no better opportunity to know and understand your partner than during conflict. How someone cares,

The Value of Conflict

what they say and their reaction during a conflict can tell more about who they are; than when everything is going well in a relationship.

When couples have conflict in their relationship, it affords them an opportunity of growing their level of trust. This will of cause be determined by the level of respect that the couples give each other during the conflict. Partners that give each other an opportunity to express opinions without shutting each other out will help to reinforce their love, as the other person will feel that their voice matters in the relationship.

Every conflict that is handled maturely gives assurance of an opportunity in the relationship to express one's feelings without feeling judged. This matured approach to conflict makes fighting and conflict in the relationship less. You have heard me right; when you handle conflict constructively; you lessen the frequency of the conflict in your relationship. Avoiding conflict can lead to bitterness in a relationship with the ability to make the relationship sour which affects the true love that a couple shares.

Disagreements in a relationship provide a couple with an opportunity to express their emotions or things that do not make them feel less valued. This helps couples to ease anxiety, tension and fears in their relationship. Anxiety and tension can have a negative impact in a relationship as it can affect communication and fun. Anxiety in a relationship can lead to suspiciousness or paranoia with the partner thinking that they are not loved, or that their partner does not care. Conflict helps to bring facts to the table, affording the couple with an opportunity to address any form of anxiety.

Conflict helps couples to know and understand each other's opinions, as things are cleared without fear or intimidation. Such a level of confidence in a relationship helps the couple to express their feelings and thoughts. Expressed feelings and thoughts in a relationship lead to an increase in intimacy.

The Value of Conflict

When you understand what the boundaries with your partner are, you can know how to deal with those boundaries to avoid escalating tensions. Couples who protect each other by knowing what hurts the other partner breeds appreciation for each other. Conflict in a relationship gives each partner an opportunity to find them and understand what is important to them as they find out what is important to their partner.

Conflict helps to develop each spouse's character, and they also gain valuable expertise and experience in handling similar matters in future. Conflict becomes an opportunity for growth as you also learn certain things about yourself that you would not have known before conflict encounters. True love which is characterised by patience toward your partner is experienced during conflict. When there is conflict, decide to care and love your partner though you might not be agreeing on certain things.

When you choose to let love lead the conflict, you come out a better and wiser person. Conflict helps you to

True Love Through Conflicts

prioritise you and your partner more than winning because you know that the health and happiness of your relationship, is of value to you as a couple.

When lovers fight

One wonders how two people who love each other can fight or have conflict. I will say it is until you have had conflict and you know that you can manage it well that you can say you are ready to get married. When lovers fight, they are looking for a common understanding on something that is important to both. We come into a relationship with our proven methods of doing things, and it might prove difficult to let go. If couples fail to agree on methods of success in handling things like money, children, time or cleanliness around the house; they might experience fights as each spouses tries to enforce their way of doing things. This can lead to more conflict which sometimes escalates into fights. What is important is how we handle conflict that will help in finding a way that a couple can agree on.

The Value of Conflict

When conflict is managed properly, it has the potential of leading a couple to a place where both spouses feel loved the way they want to be loved. It is easy for one in a relationship to do what they think is best for the relationship without getting the view of their partner. This can include things like how we spend time together as a couple and including time with children.

Someone might argue that we do not need to fight in order to agree on how we spend our time as a couple. The problem is that couples come in a relationship or marriage with certain habits that can be hard to abandon. Conflict in relationships provides an opportunity for each partner to be heard and supported when they are handled properly. When couples find an opportunity to fight or argue about something, it allows for an opportunity to iron out any differences before they become big things which can disrupt their relationship. Conflict gives a couple an opportunity to explain their needs and expectations which they may have found to be difficult to articulate.

True Love Through Conflicts

In conflict, couples fight because they love each other and want to make sure that the relationship works. Couples will fight in the relationship and still choose to stay because they believe in what they share more than what they disagree about. If the relationship is not important to the couple, they can separate even after an argument.

When fighters have conflict, it gives them an opportunity to communicate more than those who choose to ignore things that they are not happy about in a relationship. Lack of communication has been identified as the number one reason why many relationships fail work.

Communication during conflict can sound loud, harsh or confrontational but at the end of the day, it is communication. The silent couples that we perceive to be having a quiet and good marriage are more at risk of having their relationship failing because they lack communication.

The Value of Conflict

A couple will fight because they love each other and want to make their relationship work, one should be worried when their partner is no longer fighting to make the relationship work. You rather have a partner who expresses their unhappiness about something than one who pretends to like what you are saying or doing. Then, later they might come to use their banked unhappiness against you in the future. Many relationships have died a slow death because of the silence, which is brought about by the need to have peace in the relationship. Internal turmoil in a relationship is more dangerous than an external turmoil because the external turmoil can be addressed rather than the internal one.

The only way to address the internal things that affect your partner is through communication and communication comes in different ways. A couple should always seek to fight in order to bring about a solution. This should always be interpreted as a sign to say I want to make sure that our relationship works best. The ability to still want to fight to resolve any misunderstandings in the relationship is a sign that there

True Love Through Conflicts

is interest to keep the relationship going. Conflict is a good sign that shows that there are two equals in the relationship, who believe in their voice being heard in the relationship.

Boundaries in relationships

Conflict in a relationship helps couples to set boundaries. Healthy boundaries in a relationship are important for any relationship as they help in building self-esteem. Boundaries help to reflect individuality in the relationship and what you want out of the relationship. Boundaries in a relationship are important as they give your partner an opportunity to understand what is important to you and how far they can go in relation to your space and *vice versa*. Boundaries help to create a romantic space which includes physical, emotional and sexual.

In discussing boundaries, couples will talk about what they like and dislike. They will also talk about what they are comfortable with versus what scares them. The discussion of boundaries helps in identifying how you

The Value of Conflict

want to be treated in certain situations. When boundaries are not clear in a relationship, they can lead to conflict, which when managed effectively can help in setting proper and understandable boundaries. It is important that couples should clearly communicate their needs in order to avoid conflict, but we know that some things can only be addressed when they happen.

Setting boundaries helps couples to address things like the involvement of friends and families in a relationship, while creating an opportunity to talk about the role each of your careers will play in the relationship. Boundaries help to talk about the things that can cause conflict in a relationship; to be honest, most of the time, we know what is required of us.

Conflict can help to enforce the boundaries. I have dealt with several relationships which were on the brink of a breakdown because of cheating. This is one of the boundaries in a relationship that many couples do not talk about, but it tends to cause more conflicts or break relationships. It was after one partner has gone out of the

True Love Through Conflicts

boundary of the relationship between the two that they will realise the importance the other attaches to keeping the boundary between the two of them. A couple which communicates their expectations concerning boundaries avoid assumptions which can lead to more conflicts.

Power struggle in relationships

Romantic relationships mostly start with excitements which make the couples to ignore some of the wrongs the other person is doing. This is the honeymoon stage of the relationship and once this stage has settled, the couple moves from giving themselves over completely to the relationship to a state where they look for a balance. This becomes a stage where the couple will be looking for stability and security that allows them to have their autonomy back. At this stage, there can be a power struggle in the relationship which if not managed, can make the couple feel that the love, they had for each other is over.

The ability to make own choices becomes important for the future of the relationship. A power struggle in a

The Value of Conflict

relationship can be seen when both partners always want to be right where they will hold on to their idea to the extent that they stop listening to each other while refusing to hear the other party's perspective. Conflict during power struggle could make the couple know their position in the relationship and this they can achieve if they are able to manage the conflict positively. In order to manage conflict during a power struggle, it will be important for each partner not to focus only on their own interests while ignoring their partner's wishes and desires.

In building a healthy relationship through conflict, couples will need to remember that no one is perfect. Having such minds during conflict helps spouses to address each other with grace and mercy. Conflict during power struggle can help couples not to focus on each other's flaws while forgetting their own. Handled in a healthy manner, conflict helps couples not to allow current disagreements lead them to be nostalgic. Conflict can easily make partners forget all the good

True Love Through Conflicts

times and focus on the present struggles, but each struggle won creates hope for the relationship especially amid challenges.

"Peace is not absence of conflict; it is the ability to handle conflict by peaceful means"

~Ronald Reagan~

Chapter 6

❦

Handling Conflict

In order to handle conflict in a healthy manner, you will need to focus your energy in changing yourself rather than wanting your partner to change because you are part of the problem in as much as you have concluded your partner is. I have seen people who want their partners to come to marital sessions because they believe that they have a problem. It is easy to see a 'match-stick' in your partner's eyes and make noise about it, only to realise that you are carrying a log on your head. We cannot approach conflict with a self-righteous mentality because you are going to be pointing fingers

Handling Conflict

more than trying to find a good way to manage the situation.

Guiding Behaviours during Conflict:

1. Focus on the substance of the problem while keeping an eye on the relationship. (CIOS, 2018) As per the words of Roger Fisher 'be hard on the problem but be soft on the person'.

- Analyse the problem from other's point of view
- Avoid defining the substantive problem as a people problem
- Deal with emotions and people problems first
- Negotiate how to negotiate

2. Separate interest (needs) from position (demand or wants)

- Look for the needs underlying the position
- Elicit and give information

3. Develop options where both can profit

True Love Through Conflicts

- Refuse to accept the easy solution
- Examine solutions to ensure an idea really can be implemented
- Put more than one item on the table at a time so trades can be made
- Give up items which are of little interest to you but valuable to the other person

4. Evaluate many possible solutions

In order to handle conflict constructively, couples will need to adopt behaviours that are adaptive to the situation, person and issues of the moment. In handling the conflict, the couple will need to appropriately balance their interests to maximise the opportunities that come with mutual gains. When couples know each other's interests and goals they will be able to create adaption, which will afford them an opportunity to find the path that they will both be willing to walk. This will in-turn help them discover mutually acceptable outcomes. In managing conflict positively, the couple should understand that it is not just about the outcome, but the process of getting to the outcome should be considered as important.

Handling Conflict

It is not what happens to you in life or in a relationship but how you handle it that will determine the value of it. How a couple will handle conflict can either make the relationship stronger or can mean the end of the relationship. Knowing how to handle conflict in a relationship can leave you with rich social support and love. It is important for anyone in any form of relationship to learn the right conflict handling skills which can help during times of conflict.

Having these skills will be like taking insurance to cover yourself in times of need. For every couple to get the most out of their relationship, it will be important to find healthy ways of handling conflict without letting it conflict drain them. People do not handle things the same way and what I may consider a problem can be a pathway to a great solution for someone. We all face challenges in life that move us to our next level of growth. As Herresh Sippy says "conflict and resolutions are two sides of the same coin", which simply put says, where there is conflict, there is a solution and opportunity for growth for those involved.

True Love Through Conflicts

Poor conflict management skills can result in conflict producing undesired results in any relationship, while with proper skills and training a couple stands to benefit more from a conflict than the times of laughter and parties. Since it is inevitable for any relationship to face conflict, it is then important to find ways to handle conflict in a way that will bring a solution as failure to handle conflict properly can be a source of stress.

It is tempting to see a couple that has been together for many years and still happy, and assume that it is a smooth ride for them to get to where they are. In most of the time, you will be looking at two people who have been through hard times in their lives but choose to stick together. One skill that made them survive all those years was how they handled conflict in their relationship. "Behind every happy couple, lies two people who have fought hard to overcome all obstacles and interferences to be that way. Why? Because it was what they wanted" ~ Kim Genge.

Avoidance

Handling Conflict

It is not fun and exciting to have conflict and arguments with the person who claims to love you and have your best interest at heart. This results in some couples doing their best to avoid conflicts by complying with what their partner demands. Couples who normally avoid conflict risk being unhappy and resentful in their relationship. The worse things to happen when important matters that could cause conflict are avoided is that the couple starts thinking negatively and unfairly about each other. When couples have reached a stage where they are resentful towards each other, they will have more and more of unresolved important issues in their relationship which could, in turn, lead to blaming each other with no one taking responsibility for their relationship failures.

Many couples suppress their anger or just choose to get along as they think that by addressing a conflict, they will be creating one, and simply keep quiet when upset. Unfortunately, this is not a healthy long-term strategy as unresolved conflict can lead to resentment and additional unresolved conflict in a relationship. Failure for couples to handle conflict constructively can escalate conflict.

True Love Through Conflicts

John Gottman and his team studied the way couples fight and found that they can predict which couples will go on to divorce by observing their conflict resolution skills.

Negotiation

In order to be able to negotiate properly during a conflict, you will need to understand that you have an important part to play in managing the conflict; while negotiating to acknowledge your feelings and why you are feeling that way. This will help you to express the causes of conflict without attacking or undermining your spouse. You will need to be clear about what you expect from the other party so that they can agree or disagree about the possibility of making your wishes possible. It is during this time that you should be able to communicate your feelings, thoughts and expectations so that you can avoid the same conflict happening again in your relationship. Be open-minded and willing to hear what your partner has to offer as a solution to the challenge causing the conflict.

Handling Conflict

Conflict escalates when people approach the negotiations with a preconceived set of expectations without room for a different perspective or solution. If you approach conflict with the mind-set of 'knowing it all' and having all the answers, any answer given during negotiations will not suit you.

Know when conflict management is not working

Unresolved conflict in a relationship can cause more damage to the health and well-being of those involved. There are times when it will be advisable to put distance in the relationship or even to cut ties completely. In case of abuse where one's life and safety are in danger, there is no management style that should be used to continue endangering someone's life.

Gary and Carrie Oliver in their book "Mad About Us" mention seven steps to handling conflict in a relationship. In their book, Gary and Carrie encourage couples to have a plan on how they will handle conflict when it comes knocking on their door. It is not 'if but

True Love Through Conflicts

'when' because the conflict in a relationship is inevitable. They mention the seven steps to follow as:

- Define the Issue, Pray, Listen and Seek Understanding: when choosing to address the problems you are facing in your relationship avoid bringing everything at one time and things that are not relevant or related to what is on the agenda. It is important to agree about what you are going to talk about. While agreeing on the matters to be discussed do not underestimate what your partner brings to the agenda as no issue. Such behaviour will deny you the opportunity to know what your partner needs. It is important to always invite God in everything that you are doing, as that is an acknowledgement of His ability over your situation. Every communication with your partner should be driven by the need to want to understand their concern or pain than you wanting your partner to understand your pain. Seek to listen than to be listened to. There is no way you will resolve what you do not know or understand. Take time to understand the issues brought before

Handling Conflict

you and how your partner sees it without trying to correct what they are saying. Remember, to build a strong intimacy with your partner, you will need to practice the listening skills more than the talking skills. When you choose to listen to another person, you are saying that you value them and their concerns and that they are worth taking the time to understand. (Dr. Carrie, 2018) Once you feel you have understood your partner's concerns, take time to clarify if what you have heard is what they meant. Only when you feel that you have heeded and understood your partner's concerns can you seek the opportunity to identify and clarify your own core concerns.

- How important is it? Without undermining your partner's concerns as raised, we need to realise that some of the issues that cause conflict in relationships have to do with personalities or basic needs that are not being met. We need to acknowledge that there are some of the issues that we can live with while others can be resolved. Dealing with personalities can prove more of a hard task than having differences on what to eat for supper.

- Ask Yourself: What is my contribution to the problem? It is easy to see the other person's contribution to the problem we are facing but fail to see our own contribution to the situation. It is easy to quickly point out the changes that the other party needs to make to make the relationship work while we fail to identify our own short-comings. We know what the other person should change to make the best partner while we fail to acknowledge the changes we need to make. This is one sign of pride which comes before the fall, as no one will ever correct a proud person who sees everyone as wrong except themselves. Conflict is almost never about what it seems to be on the surface.
- Do I need to apologise or ask for forgiveness?
- Apologising and owning your mistakes is one key to making conflict healthy (Dr. Hall, 2017).
- Choose Radical Responsibility: you do this by making sure you take responsibility for your actions.

Handling Conflict

- Choose What You Both Can Do Differently: your partner knows best about the pain they have gone through. Take time to enquire about their suggested solution to the problem raised.
- Pray About it, do it and review it: there are certain things that are in our power to resolve, but there are those we will need heaven's intervention to resolve. While you pray about the problem you are facing in a relationship, you should seek for an opportunity to do good for your partner. Take time to ask your partner how they are feeling after a few days.

There is always an opportunity for growth in any conflict, and it is important to ask God to reveal that opportunity through prayer. Do not miss the opportunity of growing in your relationship by becoming stubborn and not willing to listen to your partner. Through introspection, the Holy Spirit can reveal the things you are not aware of about yourself. Conflict provides an opportunity for the fruit of the spirit to be fully revealed and manifested in us. A fruit are never meant to be enjoyed by the tree, but by those who have been watering the tree. Always work hard to show the true character of your faith as an ambassador of the Kingdom of God to your partner.

The appropriate way to handle conflict in a relationship is through communication. For your relationship to mature and grow stronger, it will require effective and healthy communication. Here are some of the tips as stated by "https://www.LoveisRespect.org" on how to resolve conflicts in a healthy way (Respect, 2018):

- Set Boundaries: everyone deserves to be treated with respect even during conflict. If your partner curses you, call you names or ridicules you, tell them to stop. If they do not, walk away and tell them that you do not want to continue arguing with them.
- Find the Real Issue: Typically, arguments in a relationship happen when needs are not met. Try to get to the heart of the matter. If your partner seems needy, maybe they are just feeling insecure and need your encouragement. If you're angry that your partner is not taking out the trash, maybe you are

Handling Conflict

really upset because you feel like you do all the work around the house. Learn to talk about the real issues so you can avoid constant fighting.

- Agree to Disagree: If you and your partner cannot resolve an issue, sometimes it is best to drop it. You cannot agree on everything. Focus on what matters. If the issue is too important for you to drop and you cannot agree to disagree, then maybe you are not compatible.
- Compromise If Possible: easy to say but hard to do, compromising is a major part of conflict resolution for any successful relationship. So, your partner wants Chinese food, and you want Indian. You can compromise and get Chinese on one night, but Indian the next time you eat out. Find a middle ground that can allow both of you to feel satisfied with the outcome.
- Consider Everything: Is this issue important? Does it change how the two of you feel about each other? Are you compromising your beliefs or morals? If yes, it is important that you really stress your position. If

not, maybe this is a time for compromise. Also, consider your partner's arguments. Why are they upset? What does the issue look like from their point of view? Is it unusual for your partner to get this upset? Does your partner usually compromise? Are you being inconsiderate? (Hotline, 2018).

If you are still arguing after trying all these tips but still ague constantly, consider seeking assistance from professionals to establish whether the relationship is right for both of you. Conflict in relationships in unavoidable but how we handle and negotiate during conflict can help the relationship to grow. Conflict is like compost which might not smell nice, but it helps trees to grow and bear fruits.

Handling Conflict

"Arguing -even passionately -is one of the privileges of a committed relationship. But by fighting fair you can leverage conflict towards deeper intimacy. Couples that avoid fighting also avoid making up. They do not reap the benefits of navigating a difficult issue and coming out stronger and more connected on the other side. When couples learn to fight fair, they often enjoy a deeper respect and regard for one another and enjoy happier, healthier relationships"

~Zach Brittle~

Chapter 7

୶

Destructive Conflict Management

We have learnt that conflict in itself is not as bad; sometimes it is necessary in order to provide clarity on some important elements that can help the relationship to be better and stronger. However, the way conflict is handled can create more problems in a relationship. Conflict occurs when people disagree or have different views on important issues in their relationship. Destructive conflict can quench the fire of true love and can affect other important aspects that make the relationship enjoyable.

True Love Through Conflicts

Failure to handle conflict in a healthy manner can escalate the conflict to the extent that it take control of the relationship. When that happens, it is easy for a couple to forget the good qualities they share and enjoy about each other. When conflict is poorly handled, two people can forget about the substantive issues and transform their purpose to getting even, retaliating or hurting each other. In destructive conflict encounters where one party is not happy with the outcome, and do not see themselves benefiting from the proposed solution, a spouse can decide to leave the relationship.

In destructive conflicts where one party is not happy with the outcome, because they don't see themselves benefiting from the proposed solution can leave them disgruntled. The disgruntled partner can wait for their turn to revenge. A continuation of this create relapses or a negative spiral in the relationship which affects the love that a couple shares. Conflict can become destructive when partners are rigid and competitive. Couples who fail to see their uniqueness and the value they add to each

Destructive Conflict Management

other, end up seeing each other as enemies rather than lovers.

To avoid having destructive conflict in a relationship, here are some few tips that will help:

- Avoidance: It is dangerous to keep quiet and wait until you are angry to address issue that you are not happy with in a relationship. It is possible that when you open your mouth to speak you might say things you do not mean due to anger. It becomes easy to complain to everyone in your life who will listen to your pity stories about the unjust you are going through. We fail to discuss issues that are bothering us in our relationships in a calm and respectful manner, while we go around talking to our colleagues and friends about our relationship. I always avoid being a dustbin of other people's problems especially when you expect me not to say anything to the perpetrator. It is easy to gossip about your partner under the pretence that you want to pour out

True Love Through Conflicts

your heart. It is like those people who will complain about poor service from the salon, but keep going back. When they are there, they smile and act like everything is fine, only to come and complain. You should be careful about such people because they will corrupt your thoughts about their partner, while every evening they spend cuddly nights.

When you talk to people who cannot do anything about your situation, you are increasing the pressure on yourself and your relationship. This results in increased conflict over time and inappropriate upsurge. When you avoid conflict in a relationship, you might think you are doing it for the sake of peace, but you are only living in a false peace. The more you try to avoid conflict with your partner, the more you get stressed as tensions rise. The avoidance of conflict makes you resentful, and it will be a matter of time before there are inappropriate outbursts. There is

Destructive Conflict Management

nothing that could help during conflict than addressing your partner in a respectful manner.

- Desire to Win: When you approach conflict like a competition where you feel entitled to win or to be right, you will fail to find a solution that can help your relationship to experience true love. Approaching conflict with that attitude, blinds you to real solutions or better compromises. When one gets into a relationship, they bring with them with personal experiences and exposures to situations which include realities that we value. It is important that during conflict you do not insist on your own way. Allow your partner to give their perspective on the problem; that way you stand a good chance of finding a solution you may not have thought of alone. Remember that during conflict management we do not have the 'right' or 'wrong' way because any viewpoint can be effective in solving the problem. Always show respect to your partner by finding a mutual understanding of the conflict while you both come up with a resolution that will respect each other's needs. Remember that true love is not self-seeking.

- Couples should avoid generalising, blame or to criticise one another during a conflict resolution session. Generalisation means a written or spoken statement in which one says or writes that something is true all the time when it is only true some of the times. This takes place when something happens with your partner and you do not like it by making a sweeping statement like 'you always' or 'you are like my ex' or 'you are all the same'. When you criticise your partner, you are attacking their character with statements about them, rather than an action. Every time you speak to your partner during conflict or argument and you use the statement like 'you always...' or 'you never...' please consider first if that is really the truth. Avoid bringing up past conflicts into new conflicts as this is often seen as an attempt to change the discussion to avoid

Destructive Conflict Management

taking responsibility for one's own actions or lack of engagement. Criticising your partner during conflict can be interpreted as a failure to admit to any weakness by trying to avoid the fault. The level of conflict or argument can increase when one partner or both seem to come with tactics to move away from the topic, and the arguments become attacks on the person rather than addressing the issues.

- During conflict do not try to assume or guess your partner's feelings or what is hurting them before you hear them. When you try to guess your partner's feelings it leads to poor communication and in turn, it further increases the conflict. When you do not ask, you tend to guess or assume what the other person is feeling with your own motivations than the other person's. Give your partner the right to self-determination which allows them space and time to explain their problem without interrupting them. Failure to do this takes away their voice in the relationship and more issues will not be resolved.

- When your partner does not feel heard nor listened to, it allows resentment and unresolved conflict to grow out of control. During a conflict, your body language speaks louder than anything you are saying. Approaching any conflict with contempt for your partner by making them feel worthless or beneath consideration shows that you are thinking low of them regardless of what you say with your words. Avoid actions like eye rolling, sighs and lack of listening during the conflict. Partners who are defensive during a conflict, denying any wrongdoing or work hard to avoid looking at the possibility that they could be contributors to the problem, negatively affects the resolution process. This in turn causes more destruction.

Nobody likes conflict but sweeping issues under the rug ultimately causes more damage than addressing things directly."

~ Unknown~

Chapter 8

Unresolved Conflict

Conflict unresolved in a relationship can lead to anger which can be described as a strong feeling of annoyance, displeasure, or hostility.

Unresolved or poorly managed conflict can result in eroded trust, decreased motivation about the love and feelings towards each other. This can result in increased stress and health risk on the couple. When a couple fails to manage conflict constructively or in a healthy manner, it can lead to hidden agendas and lack of communication on important things that are supposed to make true love flourish. Where there is poor or lack of communication

Unresolved Conflict

in a relationship, there are poor decisions made which in-turn affects the love that a couple shares.

Unresolved conflict in a relationship can cause physical illness as the study by Claudia Haase, found. Because anger speeds up one's heart rate and raises their blood pressure, and the more this occurs over time, it causes wear and tear on the heart, raising the risk for life-threatening heart attack problems.

Anger in a relationship is common as it becomes a valuable emotion that indicates that there are things that need to be addressed. This happens as for some people it is hard for them to understand the signal of change until there is some anger attached to the emotion. Managed anger can become the right step to solving some of the problems in a relationship. When we fail to resolve conflict in our relationships it has the potential to lead to anger. Paul in Ephesians 4: 26 -27 says:

> *"Be angry, and do not sin": do not let the sun go down on your wrath, nor give place to the devil."*

True Love Through Conflicts

Paul is clear that it is not wrong to be angry, but what you do while you are angry becomes more crucial. He warns us about the danger of anger, but at the same time, he says it is not wrong to be angry. During a conflict that is not resolved, there can be a temptation to say words or comments that are hurting. Such words or comments can last long in your spouse's mind even after you have apologised.

Failure to resolve conflict in a relationship can lead to revenge which is sometimes expressed as silent treatment. Communication is the most important asset of any relationship, and when it fails, it weakens the relationship. Using revenge during unresolved conflict can further strain the relationship. It is clear in the words of Paul when he says using revenge is tantamount to giving the 'devil' an opportunity in your relationship.

When revenge begins to show up in a relationship, you know that love has taken a serious blow as true love protects. Revenge clearly says to your partner, 'I want you to feel the pain I went through', 'I want to get back at

Unresolved Conflict

you for what you have done to me'. Unresolved conflict leads to a deep desire to want to see your partner feeling the same frustration you went through. This will be in contravention of the principle of true love which is based on the need to care and protect.

During revenge, one can construct hurtful words which we know are sensitive to hurt our partner. Once you revenge and win a round, you will always be watching your back as you will be wondering about your partner's next move for revenge.

Revenge has the potential to destroy the person who is doing the revenge than the recipient. In pursuit of teaching your partner a lesson, you might find that you are the one who will learn the greatest lesson. We can only build strong and healthy relationships when we deal with each other with compassion.

When your spouse is angry, and the matter is not resolved, it can easily lead to bitterness. Bitterness can be explained as anger and disappointment for being treated unfairly. The synonym for bitterness is resentment which can be explained as a feeling of anger when one is forced to accept someone or something that you do not like. When conflict in a relationship is not resolved, there can be a sense of injustice or wrongdoing from the individual.

A relationship that is maturing, will not run short of offences and that should tell us that when you do get into a relationship, you must have a forgiving heart. During bitterness in a relationship one writes off their partner's suggestions too quickly and can also prevent the partner to have a constructive conversation. The worst thing that bitterness can do is to damage your self-esteem, as you will start seeing yourself as less adequate for your partner. Self-doubt leads to you failing to express your feelings in the relationship.

Prolonged conflict and badly managed conflict in relationships raises hormone levels which can result in psychological stress. This weakens the immune system making one to be more susceptible to viral infections. In order to reduce physical stress during a conflict, couples need to concentrate on the issues that are discussed or

Unresolved Conflict

put on the agenda at that time. This will help to reduce the level of arguments during a conflict. Conflict in relationships is not bad but sarcasm, name-calling and backbiting creates problems that can prolong conflict.

Unresolved conflict or poorly managed conflict leaves a couple emotionally drained and exhausted. Due to the psychological impact of conflict on the mind of those involved, , a couple can find that the level of anxiety impairs their ability to concentrate, which then affects their performance in other areas of life. When conflict is prolonged and unconcealed, a couple's true love functions at a sub-optimal level.

Failure to manage conflict constructively can lead to mental issues as conflict elicits stress which is a self-guarding device against destructive elements in our world. Stress is produced in our body to warn us of any form of danger. When the stress level is always high because of the pressures we experience in our relationships, it can lead to psychological problems which might include anxiety disorders and depression.

True Love Through Conflicts

The other important thing to remember is that stress borne from conflict can make a couple feel distrust, anger, anxiety and fear, which in turn can destroy true love in a relationship. When conflict is not openly addressed but avoided, many issues can be left unresolved which in turn fuel feelings of resentment and anger.

Unresolved Conflict

"If you come to a negotiation table saying you have the final truth, that you know nothing but the truth and that is final, you will get nothing."

~Harri Holkeri~

Chapter 9

ঌ

Negotiating Conflicts

The dictionary (which dictionary?) defines negotiation as a process to find a way over or through an obstacle or difficult route. Negotiation can also be explained as having a formal discussion with someone in order to reach an agreement with them. Couples come together with different goals and ambitions through love that joins them. To make the relationship grow to their benefit, couples will have to negotiate and pursue each other. This will be achieved when a couple includes either compromise or a better way forward to address their needs.

True Love Through Conflicts

When a couple compromises, no one gets what they want as they try to find a middle ground, which ends up making neither of them happy. Negotiations in a relationship provide a better solution than compromise. During the negotiation, you learn to give up something that you really want for something that your partner really wants. The idea behind giving up what you want for your spouse is to make sure that you contribute to the relationship. This allows you to give your partner an opportunity to give something in return into the relationship.

Relationships require couples to have negotiation skills because both have opinions and rights that should be respected. Negotiation becomes important in a relationship because a couple's goals and ambitions will not always be the same. It is important to know that during negotiation, you will have a win-lose outcome. In as much as compromise is important, a couple needs to learn negotiating skills.

Negotiating Conflicts

When there is always one person in a relationship who feels that they must always compromise for the sake of peace, it leads to where their voice is no longer heard. In compromising, one might do things for the sake of peace, failing to express their feelings. This, in a long-run, may to lead to resentment. Negotiations in a relationship give a couple an opportunity to uncover each other's hidden interest.

During negotiations with your partner, you should always choose to listen with an open mind. You will show this by the way you ask questions and actively listening to your partner's views. Failure to listen to your partner empathetically will result in them being hostile toward what you have to offer, no matter how good it might be. The important element for any negotiation should be, trust. In negotiating with your partner, make sure that you acknowledge their concerns and the proposed solution without shutting them out. In acknowledging their point and their view, you are reaffirming that you have heard their concerns and also that you are ready to address them.

True Love Through Conflicts

When you shut their point, and you do not acknowledge your partner's views, you are creating an environment where they will need to defend their view. This might result in a long process in which none of you might see the value in each other's proposed solution. In your negotiations, make sure you create a two-way communication, as this will make sure that your partner feels part of the process.

This could further be shown by asking for clarity, seeking questions, which will clearly show that you want to understand your partner's point of view. Talking with your partner with respect and willingness to listen, affords them an opportunity to respond in the same manner. Social science has proven that people tend to respond to others' actions with similar actions.

To avoid a situation where you are on a vicious cycle which is filled with contention and suspicions, evade a situation where your partner feels that they must guard themselves while competing for their voice to be heard. Negotiations between couples can prove to be difficult

Negotiating Conflicts

and challenging when there has been a level of mistrust in the relationship.

When you approach your partner to negotiate, make sure that you have addressed the important issues that you know you are responsible for in your relationship. Make sure you show interest in your partner's well-being days before you can even start negotiating. This might sound like bribery, but it is always important to prepare the ground before you could plant the seed. Even the seed itself needs to be prepared before going to the ground; otherwise, you might waste a good seed on wrongly prepared soil.

Know yourself to know what you need

During a conflict with your partner, you need to know what has hurt you and how it hurts. Remember that these are your feelings, and no one should try to explain them better than you. It is important when you are approaching your partner to negotiate through the conflict knowing and understanding yourself and your needs. Many of the conflicts that couples go through can be resolved through the process of negotiation. Negotiation helps couples avoid many of the unnecessary conflicts as during negotiation, they learn to 'win some and lose some'. This, in turn, gives the couple an opportunity to have their needs addressed in the relationship. Negotiation affords the couple an opportunity to get something in exchange for giving something their partner needs. When you approach your partner to negotiate an important matter of concern, you need to look within yourself and assess your own temperaments, strengths, weaknesses, insecurities, fears and internal triggers.

This self-awareness and self-knowledge will give you an opportunity to self-control and to focus on what is important to you. When you know yourself, and what you want out of a negotiation, you will be non-reactive in the face of unexpected reaction or provocative behaviours from your partner. During negotiations with your partner, reflect on things that give you the power to negotiate; do not allow the thought of inferiority to overshadow your negotiations. Failure to reflect on your

Negotiating Conflicts

power sources will lead to you agreeing to something that you are not happy about. If you are dealing with a partner that loses temper, or is patronising during the negotiations, always reflect on why the person's behaviour catches up with you. Always allow love to conquer any form of negotiation you are having with your partner. During the negotiation, you will find that there are signals that indicate you are going into a 'flight or fight,' mode. Some of the signals might include increased heart rate, shallow breathing, shortness of breath, perspiration, tense body muscles, etc.

When this happens, you will need to ask yourself why you are feeling that way and take the necessary actions to find relief. Some of the simple steps you can take during or when this happens include taking a deep breath or asking for a break or asking that things be slowed down so that you can both hear and understand the issues talked about during the negotiation. In your preparation to negotiate with your partner, develop a plan that helps you to remain calm or give you an opportunity to respond in an assertive, non-reactive way.

True Love Through Conflicts

While you negotiate, do not allow yourself to be verbally abused or physically intimidated. If there is something that is said or done during the negotiation that you do not like or appreciate; name it and give a clear warning that you will walk away if it continues. Always remember that you teach people how to treat you and whatever you allow will continue. When you feel that your partner is pressurising you to decide, and that you do not feel ready to make the decision, name it and suggest an alternative.

Negotiating for love to win

The main idea behind negotiating during conflict is to manage conflict between two people. During the negotiation, different opinions are considered, and this will include the individual needs, aims, interests and variances in upbringing and culture. Conflict happens

Negotiating Conflicts

because there are different opinions or views to a matter or subject. Your wish when you present your opinions is for your partner to buy into them and failure to achieve that can lead to conflict. During the negotiation, you can either approach with the mindset of "getting your own way", "driving a hard bargain" or "beating off the opponent". Approaching negotiations with your partner with this attitude can make you win the conflict while you lose your true love. Winning at all cost during a romantic relationship increases the likelihood of the relationship breaking down, and hampering the chances for reconciliation. When you engage with the competitive attitude of Win-Lose negotiation, you decide about what you want to achieve, and you take the extreme position to win at all cost. During the Win-Lose negotiation, both sides will try to hide their real views and mislead the other.

The best negotiation strategy is a Win-Win approach, which involves looking for resolutions that allow both partners in the relationship to gain. As a couple in a romantic relationship, you work together towards finding a solution to your differences that results in both sides being satisfied. The Win-Win approach emphasises preserving the relationship by separating the person from the problem. Having an attitude where you want true love to win over the differences, both parties focus on the interests, not on position.

When the focus of the negotiation during conflict is on maintaining true love, you can generate a variety of options that offer gains to both parties before deciding what to do. (Need, 2018). When you choose love to win during a negotiation, you are simply not allowing the disagreements to damage the true love you share as a couple. Couples allow each other to win during conflict negotiation because they see the future together, but when there is no future ahead winning at all cost becomes the norm.

The most important thing to remember during romantic conflict negotiations is that we negotiate to find an agreeable solution to a problem, but not an excuse to undermine each other. For the couple in negotiations to

Negotiating Conflicts

achieve this, it will be important for them to consciously separate the issues under dispute, from the person involved. What I am talking about here is 'I still love you,' 'hold you in deep regard', 'respect your worth but still disagree with you.' In all romantic conflict negotiations, it will be important to always express the love you have for each other even when you are disagreeing.

While you negotiate out of love, avoid personal confrontation by blaming your partner for creating the problem. Lastly, it will be important to always consider the emotional needs of your partner as you seek to understand his/her perspective and underlying interests during negotiations. This you can achieve by discussing how your partner feels during the negotiations.

Assertiveness in Negotiating Conflict

Assertiveness means being confident and forceful in your behaviour. This allows you to minimise stress as you can articulate yourself efficiently. You can stand up for your point of view, while also respecting the rights and beliefs of others. Negotiation is all about communication and being assertive is a core communication skill. Being in love with someone who is assertive eliminates several unnecessary conflicts that can eat into your true love.

Being assertive shows that you have respect for yourself as you are willing to stand up for your interests while expressing your thoughts and feelings. In doing this, you prove to the person you are in negotiation with that you are aware of their rights and are willing to work on resolving the conflict. The goal during negotiations is to state your problem and propose what you think will be the solution to the problem. Being assertive will grant you the best chance of successfully delivering your message in a direct and respectful way.

Passive behaviour in any romantic relationship does not mean humility. Being passive may actually be nervousness. Those who are passive in a relationship are easy to concede to whatever the other person is saying to avoid conflict. When you choose to be passive during negotiations with your partner you are simply saying your

Negotiating Conflicts

thoughts and feelings do not matter like that of your partner.

The more you try to keep the peace during negotiations by agreeing to things you are not happy about you are poisoning your relationship. It will be a matter of time before you cause internal conflicts as your needs in the relationship will come second. Internal conflict in a romantic relationship can cause stress, resentment, seething anger, feelings of victimisation and desire to exert revenge.

Learning to be assertive can take time and practice but continue expressing your true feelings and needs. The more you do this, the better you become in negotiating, and you will learn that in negotiating, true love wins.

A relationship is an investment that will build as you continue to devote your time and effort. The more you put in, the more you'll get back

~Sumesh Nair quotes~

Chapter 10

Coaching in Relationships and True Love

Relationship Coaching can be explained as a process where the principles of professional coaching to personal and business are applied to your relationship. Relationship coaching can be applied early in the relationship while the intention to help the functional couple achieve their personal and relationship goals. The coaching process in a relationship is not to solve problems or resolve the conflict, but to make sure that couples are able to set up a vision and set goals for their relationship at an early stage. As a skilful person in the relationship, the relationship coach uses the art and science of coaching to facilitate success from inside the client without providing advice or professional opinions. During the coaching, a couple will receive the support that will help them to have a successful or fulfilled relationship.

Relationship coaching is a result and goal-oriented method that accepts that the couples seeking the services of a coach, are fully efficient and capable to make the relationship a success. Working with the couple, the relationship coach will rather focus on the strength and abilities that the couple must make the relationship a success. This could be different from going through psychotherapy where a trained and licensed professional diagnoses and treats mental, emotional, and psychological disorders. Working with someone who is a coach and professional therapist can be helpful as coaching will continue from where therapy ends with the focus of personal growth.

Coaching in Relationships and True Love

The key aspect of a couple's coaching is assessing and adapting day-to-day conducts to apprehend the results you want in the future. This is done under the principle that says the future we want tomorrow starts today. True love is not a wish but a desire that should be fuelled by a daily conscious decision to make love win at all cost. Couple coaching helps the clients to get clear measurable results in order to achieve this goal. This could include steps taken to address or manage problems that couples know that they are hurting the relationship in order to create a brighter future.

Value of Relationship Coach

Using the service of a relationship coach will help the couple to tap into a unique and powerful platform which has the potential to help them find fulfilment in life and relationship. Relationships are the most important part of our daily lives, especially romantic relationship, as it can help to bring meaning, comfort and happiness in one's life. A romantic relationship impacts more on your emotional well-being which if not managed properly can

True Love Through Conflicts

affect many other areas of your life. A good romantic relationship provides love, support, happiness, friendship, advice and guidance. When you understand that your success and quality of life is directly associated with the quality of your relationship, you will make sure you invest in building a fulfilling relationship. True love taken for granted or misused, can affect the way you will relate with any person in the future who claims to love you.

Any break-up of a romantic relationship can cause problems and emotional turmoil. Using the services of a coach will assist in making sure that you are guided in your intention of having a fulfilling relationship. Coaching will help you identify what you want out of a romantic relationship and how you will identify that which you desire from the relationship. Working with a relationship coach assists you to move further and faster towards your goals than you could do on your own. Having a coach gives you access to a wealth of knowledge and skills you need as you will realise that you do not know what you do not know. The future success of your

Coaching in Relationships and True Love

relationship depends on access to new relationship skills and knowledge which your coach will be able to provide. Relationship coaches work from the view that every person they work with already knows how to make positive choices and to take the necessary action to have a successful relationship.

With this knowledge, the relationship coach will work with you to make sure that you are ready for action in your relationship. Through the guidance of the relationship coach, you are in the process of self-awareness and learning on how to make relationship choices that will sustain your true love. The ability to identify what you want from a relationship will help you not to settle for less or risk preventable failures.

To achieve this, you will need to make sure that you give yourself the necessary support to be successful, and a coach can come in handy in helping you to find that fulfilment. During the relationship coaching sessions, the coach will assist you to be authentic with yourself, by making sure that you do not settle for less than you really wanted. This the coach will achieve by being a sounding board and providing the necessary 'reality checks.' As the vision and the goals of your relationship become clear, the relationship coach will then be able to assist you on how to be active in managing conflicts or problems in their early stages. As we grow, we have ambitions and dreams that we, over time, start to doubt and lose the momentum towards them. Because the relationship coach holds the highest vision for you beyond your fears and limitations, their role will be to make sure you go beyond your limitations.

Mediation during a conflict

Mediation can be explained as a process where a neutral third party assists disputing parties in resolving conflict using specialised communication and negotiation techniques. It is during this process where all the parties are encouraged to participate as the role of the mediator to manage the interaction between parties and facilitate open communication. Mediation can be looked at as a process to get another person involved in the love life of two people meaning confidentiality is more important during the time of mediation.

During my research, I have found that couples would use the services of a mediator in their conflict when there is a conflict they are failing to resolve. In most of the cases, the couple will prefer to use their friends, church leaders, family members and as last option the couple will go to a professional (psychologist/social worker). A mediator can be someone that the couple trusts and respects. This helps in maintaining order during conflict.

During conflict, the mediator helps the couple to be in control of how they both like to manage the conflict in their best interest. When a couple arrives at an agreed solution, they are more likely to work together on a mediated agreement. With the help of the mediator, a couple can work mutually toward a resolution. Couples who are willing to allow the intervention of a mediator, are ready to move their position as a sign to want to work through the relationship. Allowing the mediator into their relationship says that the couple is more open-minded to understanding the other party's side and are willing on underlying issues that led to a dispute.

When such an attitude towards conflict is achieved, there is a greater possibility of preserving the relationship than when a couple tries to manage the conflict on their own. Most of the mediators we tend to use are not trained, but we prefer them because of the relationship and respect we have for them. This can sometimes leave the couple vulnerable, as some of the people we prefer to seek mediation from, might not be able to understand the value of professional conduct like 'confidentiality'.

Mediators are supposed to act neutral facilitators who guide the parties through the process of conflict. During mediation, couples are helped to think 'outside of the box' for possible solutions to the conflict, allowing them to broaden the range of possible solutions. This is another professional attribute that those who are skilled are taught to understand that every person has the right to make their own decision about the future they want for themselves. Mediation should always aim to conclude with an agreement rather than a winner or loser.

A couple will be encouraged to agree on a solution that will be seen to benefit them both than being one-sided. I have found that most couples prefer to choose their friends to mediate during conflict because of the responsiveness of the mediator in allowing the parties to come up with their own solution without strict rules. Amongst many African couples who have had *lobola* negotiators involved in their marriage, I have found that few would like to have the negotiators involved as mediators when conflict arises.

When *Lobola* negotiators are family members, they may be perceived as biased when they mediate between a fighting couple. Mediation should always allow for each party involved in the relationship to prove their self-determination and autonomy. This will require the couple to choose the area of agreement together rather than giving the power to someone outside to make the decision.

True Love Through Conflicts

References

References

CIOS, 2018. *http://www.cios.org.* [Online]
Available at: http://www.cios.org/encyclopedia/conflict/Cnature5_mutualgains.htm
[Accessed 01 December 2018].

Dictionary, C., 2018. *https://dictionary.cambridge.org/dictionary/english/ethic.* [Online]
Available at: https://dictionary.cambridge.org/dictionary/english/ethic
[Accessed 03 07 2018].

Dr. Carrie, G., 2018. *Before Conflict Arises in Marriage - MM #352 - Marriage ....* [Online]
Available at: https://marriagemissions.com/before-conflict-arises-marriage-mm-352/
[Accessed 15 December 2018].

Dr. Gary, C., 2018. *Things I Wish I'd Known Before We Got Married.* [Online]
Available at: https://maritalintimacyinst.com/wp-content/uploads/2018/04/Premarriage-What-I-Wish-Id-Known-highlights-Gary-Chapman.pdf
[Accessed 01 December 2018].

Dr. Hall, E. D., 2017. *Why Conflict Is Healthy for Relationships | Psychology Today.* [Online]
Available at: https://www.psychologytoday.com/us/blog/conscious-communication/201703/why-conflict-is-healthy-relationships
[Accessed 01 December 2018].

Hotline, T. N. D. V., 2018. *Healthy Conflict Resolution | The National Domestic ....* [Online]
Available at: https://www.thehotline.org/healthy-relationships/healthy-conflict-resolution/
[Accessed 01 December 2018].

Need, S. Y., 2018. *Negotiation in Action: Win-Win and Win-Lose | SkillsYouNeed.* [Online]
Available at: https://www.skillsyouneed.com/ips/negotiation2.html
[Accessed 15 December 2018].

Relationship, 2018. *Relationship – Page 2 – More Than Love Story.* [Online]
Available at: https://morethanlovestory.com/category/relationship/page/2/
[Accessed 01 December 2018].

Respect, L. i., 2018. *Loveisrespect.org..* [Online]
Available at: https://www.loveisrespect.org/healthy-

References

relationships/conflict-resolution/
[Accessed 01 December 2018].

Vinney, C., 2018. *Understanding Maslow's Theory of Self-Actualization.* [Online]
Available at: https://www.thoughtco.com/maslow-theory-self-actualization-4169662
[Accessed 24 January 2019].

About the Author

~Andrew Spaumer~

Andrew Spaumer is the child of God, married to Nomsa Spaumer. He is blessed with two children Nontobeko and Mofenyi. He is an international relationship counsellor, life couch, author, advanced social worker based in UK, property investor and a senior pastor at Elbethel church.

He holds a Master's degree in social work from University of Pretoria, He researched on the topic "Conflict Management in Black African Marriages" the study he completed early 2018. He holds a Diploma Life Coaching from United Kingdom.

References

He uses his life experiences to draw relationship lessons and devoted to transforming lives through relationships and marriage coaching.

www.ingramcontent.com/pod-product-compliance
Lightning Source LLC
Chambersburg PA
CBHW031356040426
42444CB00005B/308